Britain as a Special Case:

The case for Britain remaining as a member of the EU is widely misunderstood.

Members of government and the media, as well as our European partners, judge Britain on political and economic markers and conveniently ignore cultural dimensions.

The UK is a magnet for those who realise English language is a first-class ticket to a better life. Even immigrants from the poorest countries know that if they can get to England, whatever the risk, the ability to speak English is valued most, above all others.

At the other end of the scale, any established professional, academic, diplomat, musician, writer, actor or business man knows that, to be taken seriously, knowledge both of language and the English culture is essential.

Any serious scientific contribution to world knowledge is written in, or translated into, English. The media knows this, business knows this, the scientific community knows this.

Finance, medicine, computing, the political world; anyone with a knowledge of world culture and a need to communicate knows that they have to know the English language.

Paradoxically, English is now the (unofficial) 'lingua franca' of the EU, a fact consistently denied or ignored by European politicians, diplomats and functionaries. In the World, in diplomacy, in business, in economics and in science English is the world's primary language.

Mandarin (or perhaps more accurately the Han dialect) may be claimed as the language spoken by the largest number of people. This is because China has the largest population. But the language (second language included), spoken by around 1,440,000,000 people, is English. The population of the EU is around 400, million. Anyone who is anyone in Europe speaks English.

In academia, journalism, electronic media, aviation, shipping, commerce, banking and finance, education and tourism English is the foremost language, the essential language. It is the language of international broadcast media, press, entertainment, music and film and the service industry

Harvard, Yale, Melbourne, New York, Amsterdam, Paris, Tokyo, Sydney, Stanford, Hong Kong; top universities throughout the world all know that a paper written in English gains instant access to a world culture in science and technology, in medicine, law, economics and business studies. Academia across the World speaks English.

WE ARE NO "POOR RELATION"

THEY NEED US – BUT **WE** DON'T NEED THE EU.

Let us stop fooling ourselves that we are somehow Europe's poor relation, a distant cousin or a hanger-on. Britain is not only at the world's cultural core, we are the source and fountain-head of the democratic freedoms the world has come to value most. The founding fathers of America were from Britain. The Commonwealth of Nations numbers the greatest variety of peoples and independent Nations, more than any other Global institution. At its centre is Britain and the Commonwealth, Her Majesty Queen Elizabeth II the titular head.

In cultural terms, Britain leads the world as a reservoir of valued attitudes and the means to express them. Our system of government and our financial institutions and our currency are respected throughout the world, as models for other nations to build upon.

Britain formulated core freedoms and democratic values in the Magna Carta, written in 1340. By contrast, the nations of Europe, the constituent members of the EU are new-comers; neither France, Italy or Germany was even a recognizable country until the Nineteenth Century.

WE DON'T NEED TO PLEAD FOR SOVEREIGNTY – WE ALREADY HAVE IT.

In 1940 Germany was a political and financial disaster, Reconstruction relied on US funding. At the beginning of the twentieth century, with Europe in ruins, only Britain remained a free, democratic, stable and respected country, also owing a deep debt and gratitude to its closest ally, the United States.

Europe today takes on the increasing burden of economic chaos occasioned by lack of sovereign governance over its artificial currency - the hastily invented, ill-thought-out Euro.

In an attempt to invent a currency out of nothing, it now faces the chaos of enforcing artificial values on its member states, with an equally artificial central bank. Economic fault lines are obvious; German GDP cannot compensate for Greece, France for Portugal, or Denmark for Italy. Will Turkey become a part of Europe? Who governs? A Euro-club of extravagantly-paid time-servers has a vested interest in making sure it survives, despite the cost, despite the intellectual, political and cultural fault lines, despite the wilful destruction of local traditions and commerce.

Europe faces the chaos of defining its borders, having falsely led nations outside to believe they can be 'core players'. Now it finds the 'open-border' policy unworkable, un-enforceable and in direct opposition to the security of its members. The integrity of the cultural, linguistic, and economic structure of member nations is already severely compromised.

The United Kingdom already has its defined borders, it's sovereignty *and* its currency. We have an identity and a culture. Euro-land wants this to disappear. Do we really want to sacrifice our long-fought-for culture, our precious and unique identity for the bland, blank and meaningless world of Brussels and Strasbourg?

Our true cultural allies are The US, Australia and New Zealand and the Commonwealth of Nations.

Fact: The City of London is the most productive region in the E.U.

Britain and the United Kingdom represent a presence that is both long-established and respected in the World. Across the globe we are a valued partner, an authoritative voice in business, diplomacy, and law, trusted in finance, science and technology. No other European country can emulate this, nor can even the EU in its entirety. Inner London alone has a GDP of 325% of the EU average. No one else comes close. Luxemburg is next at 258% and (surprise, surprise,) then Brussels at 207% - headquarters for the EU itself, home to some of the 33,000 best-paid personnel in Europe, EU workers and officials.

Top Expertise and Productivity; the UK is Europe's Special Case

No serious scientific or academic paper, no diplomatic communiqué written in any other language than English has such world-wide credibility or scope. That is the measure of the influence of the UK. It is this stature, continuity and standards that Europe would prefer to see diminished, diluted, and hopefully dispensed with.

The UK has tried compliance, implicitly required of a member nation. But each concession provokes further demands. This is true for all member nations, yet concessions gain no reciprocal or sympathetic response in Europe. The bureaucracy in Strasburg and Brussels represent no national interest but only a bureaucratic system producing legislation merely to justify its existence. The evidence points to a pressing need to curb its legislative powers and appetites.

It has taken just a few decades for the EU bureaucracy to reveal its empty philosophy, devoid of sound economic or geopolitical principles. The EU is 'not fit for purpose' and the real purpose is now obscure and its supporting principles deeply flawed.

Leaving will not hurt the UK if separation is complete and final. But it will hurt the EU – that is what Europe fears; other member states will follow the UK's lead.

There are countless examples to illustrate the inherent problems, not flimsy 'scare stories' from the wilder fringes of the media, but actual cases from among a documented history of thousands of blunders, endless inconsistencies and serious errors. They reveal the byzantine thinking behind the World's largest bureaucratic institution outside China.

Whereas China is one nation, the EU is a cobbled-together, unwieldy, undemocratic pseudo-state.

'Waiting in the wings'; eight more supplicant nations. Like nations before them, they too, have economic woes. For them, as before, it is easier to bundle their debts together with those of the EU, carefully hiding the true scale, effectively hiding them. Once they become members, they believe, their economic problems will disappear (at least, 'off their books') and the EU tax-paying population will shoulder the burden.

The 'Enlargement' Process:

1. Turkey   - moving slowly. Recent funds transfer from EU 'compensates' Turkey for refugees in an effort to stem the tide of migrants fleeing Syria, the Middle-East and Africa. A deeply troubled nation.

2. Albania   - granted 'Candidate' status in 2014. Initial application had a dubious reception

Waiting in the wings...

3. Bosnia and Herzegovina   4. Kosovo

5. Montenegro.   6. Serbia   7.Macedonia

Does this look viable ?

Here's what Commissioner Johannes Hahn said: *"Our firm commitment to EU enlargement and to the conditions it involves is a long-term investment in Europe's own security and prosperity, ..a clear European perspective gradually transforms our partner countries.."* (Brussels. 10th November 2015).

He did not say 'countries could follow their own path' or that 'they could work to change the EU', rather the reverse.

Then there are the practical 'nuts and bolts' of EU policy. Like fishing - pertinent to Great Britain's case:

"Cod mislabelling proved more severe in Ireland than in the UK" (EU mislabelling running at over 20% - Ireland 28.4%, versus UK mislabelling at 7.4 %) "..cheaper species sold as cod or threatened Atlantic cod as 'sustainably-sourced Pacific Cod' " (Fish and Fisheries 15 July 2011 'Seafood Miss-labelling' Vol 13 issue 3. Sept 2012 Miller, Jessel and Mariani).

We play by the rules: Nobody else does.

Issues of fish quotas are still unresolved. Like Czechoslovakia's claim for a sizeable fish quota, even though it has no coastline.

There are "growing concerns about the political and geographical marginalisation of the fishing industry. To avoid social and economic isolation of our fishing industry, major steps are needed in 'no take' protection". (Marine Policy Vol. 33 iss. 5 Sept 2009 Stojanovic, Smith and Wooldridge).

Then there's farming and GM crops: there's concern that 'individual governments' are devising their own "precautionary measures", (outside the normal EU regulatory parameters). This has caused 'intense controversy.' (Journal of Risk Research. GM in the EU. Vol.3 iss3 2000).

" Compliance will require more investment"

(The Integrated Pest Management Directive:Crop Protection Vol 31 iss 1 Jan 2012).

The authoritative 'Geojournal' commented dryly ;

"Article 6 of the Habitats Directive may take a highly technocratic approach to environmental management with resultant burdens in bureaucracy". (Geojournal Vol 65 , 2006)

Other fault lines in environment, agriculture and animal welfare issues are legion; endless directives are followed by endless papers. The former are published as dictates, the latter voices are ignored; the bureaucrats have spoken, written a directive, they are not to be gainsaid. The fault-lines and discrepancies are legion, the facts make nonsense of the theory, adding to confusion and the complexity of resolution, especially for commerce, agriculture and industry.

Animal welfare:

Cattle raised in Southern France are destined, after road transport across thousands of kilometres to Italy, by directive to be slaughtered in a designated abattoir. There can be no deviation, no other market, even if there is one closer.

" The EU started discussion on animal welfare in the 1980's and adopted a series of Directives to protect animals. Animal welfare law across Europe (with) Northern States generally having the most stringent legislation"

(Applied Animal Behaviour. Science 1, vol115, iss 4., Oct 2008).

In other words, since 1980, despite directives, no standard has been achieved, despite costly, lengthy, inter-member transfers of huge numbers of animals at incalculable cost and suffering.

WE CARE ABOUT ANIMALS.

WHAT ABOUT HUMANS?

Horrors stories surrounding EU human rights legislation are a running sore, undermining pretended respect for the rule of law. Political self- righteousness from the EU makes a mockery of justice; the 'right to vote' for prisoners whose 'rights' have been abused plus the right to radicalise others, under threat from violent militants in jail in the name of 'religious belief'. Scores of cases blemish the very ideas of freedom and justice, twisted out of any recognisable shape by EU-funded legal experts.

Each EU department issues directives, non-stop: Here they are:

- Agency for the Cooperation of Energy Regulators (ACER)

- Body of European Regulators for Electronic Communications (BEREC)
- Community Plant Variety Office (CPVO)
- European Agency for Safety and Health at Work (EU-OSHA)
- European Agency for the Management of Operational Cooperation at the External Borders (FRONTEX)
- European Agency for the operational management of large-scale IT systems in the area of freedom, security and justice (eu-LISA)
- European Asylum Support Office (EASO)
- European Aviation Safety Agency (EASA)
- European Banking Authority (EBA)
- European Centre for Disease Prevention and Control (ECDC)
- European Centre for the Development of Vocational Training (Cedefop)
- European Chemicals Agency (ECHA)
- European Environment Agency (EEA)
- European Fisheries Control Agency (EFCA)
- European Food Safety Authority (EFSA)
- European Foundation for the Improvement of Living and Working Conditions (EUROFOUND)
- European GNSS Agency (GSA)
- European Institute for Gender Equality (EIGE)
- European Insurance and Occupational Pensions Authority (EIOPA)
- European Maritime Safety Agency (EMSA)
- European Medicines Agency (EMA)
- European Monitoring Centre for Drugs and Drug Addiction (EMCDDA)
- European Police College (CEPOL)
- European Police Office (EUROPOL)
- European Public Prosecutor's Office (in preparation) (EPPO)
- European Railway Agency (ERA)
- European Securities and Markets Authority (ESMA)
- European Training Foundation (ETF)
- European Union Agency for Fundamental Rights (FRA)

- European Union Agency for Network and Information Security (ENISA)
- Office for Harmonisation in the Internal Market (OHIM)
- Single Resolution Board (SRB)
- The European Union's Judicial Cooperation Unit (EUROJUST)

- T European Defence Agency (EDA)

- European Union Institute for Security Studies (EUISS)
- European Union Satellite Centre (Satcen)

- Consumers, Health, Agriculture and Food Executive Agency (CHAFEA)

- Education, Audiovisual and Culture Executive Agency (EACEA)
- European Research Council Executive Agency (ERC Executive Agency)
- Executive Agency for Small and Medium-sized enterprises (EASME)
- Innovation & Networks Executive Agency (INEA)
- Research Executive Agency (REA)

- EURATOM Supply Agency (ESA)
- European Joint Undertaking for ITER and the Development of Fusion Energy (Fusion for Energy)

- Translation Centre for the Bodies of the European Union (CdT)

We can take this last in the list as an example:

This agency employs 350 full-time translators and 400 freelancers, need to translate from all languages into all others. If necessary (and it often is) from Estonian into Maltese, then back into Estonian or Spanish, etc., etc., etc.

Translation cost **per day €118,000**. English alone costs €8,900 per day, just for France and Germany – and of course there are 28x28 possible combinations.

The logical solution is to make English (the most widely spoken language) the official language of the EU. This is anathema to all countries and is rejected.

As is the abandonment of Strasbourg as an EU centre; each month EU business witches from Brussels to Strasbourg and back again. Practically all member states recognise the waste: €200, 000,000 is spent maintaining twin centres and €113, 800,000 is spent journeying between the two, involving 1st class travel, flights, cars rail fares and hotels. Despite the objections, France has a veto: a €200 million saving year is out of the question – Strasbourg will never be abandoned as long as France has a veto, demanding EU representation must be present on French soil. 20,000 tonnes of CO_2 contaminates the European air every year because of French intransigence.

What happened to Departments for 'Disease Prevention and Control, 'Environment' or 'Safety and Health'?

Even the EU itself condemned the Union in a 2001 report (Financial Times May 16 2003) when the EU Fraud Office (OLAF) called one of its main Directorates:

"A vast enterprise for looting community funds"

In total, 34 different Directorates plus associated infrastructure, employing 33,000 people. This figure does not include the personnel necessary in individual nations or the representatives and their staff.

We can imagine how complex the structure of the EU is. Member countries spread across Europe with a myriad of different customs and languages, economies and cultures; departments in each of those countries dealing with the EU. Departments and civil servants translate Directives to enable each enactment to be implemented and policed. Delegates hired and appointed, assistants hired and accommodated in hotels while they try to sort out the complications carefully constructed in order to be deconstructed elsewhere. Thirty-Three Directorates, each with its own hierarchy of high-grade to low grade staff, offices, buildings managers, cleaners, cafes, accountants, linguists, printers, writers, telephonists, computer operators, etc; enough to represent a government of equivalent or comparable size in thirty three countries. These centres of activity change regularly, migrating between two main centres on a regular basis.

The odd thing is that each country member could just as well manage all these things in its own existing governmental structure. The EU is actually irrelevant, a bureaucratic chimera, invented by itself for itself and justifying its existence by creating more directives daily. The EU simply duplicates all the structures of member countries, then charges for the privilege.

We can imagine, should consider seriously, that if all the Directives were agreed upon and put in place, there would be no longer any need for the Brussels engine. Except the EU can't stop; it would die. Indeed, it can be demonstrated the EU is actually a brake on growth for its members. Those most integrated find it hard to grow. The fastest growth was shown by Ireland – an EU member – but from a very low base, to show 5.4% growth in 2014. Britain is also doing well; growth for the same period was 2.9%, while Germany's growth was 1.6% and the EU average 0.9 %

Do we really want to be hitched to this particular lumbering wagon? Would anyone work for, or buy anything from, the EU if it was a commercial organisation? Would you employ them? Well, you do.

How can there be any further growth if members waiting to join will simply hide dubious finances under the European 'rug'?

What about the scare that we'll suddenly lose our trading status with the rest of the world? The rest of the world already trades with the EU. Major markets are, in first place, the US, next China and then Russia. It is really feasible that if we leave the EU, these countries will, by some EU device or by some self-imposed restriction, cease trading with the UK? That proposition is ludicrous. Rather it is the EU that is wary of the special position Britain holds in world trade, finance, diplomacy and strategic alliances.

The total population breakdown for the EU is as follows:

Germany+	81,174,000
France+	66,352,469
UK+	64,767,115
Italy+	60,795,612
Poland	38,005,614
Romania+	19,861,408
Netherlands+	16,900,726
Belgium+	11,258,434
Greece+	10,812,467
Czech Rep+	10,538,275
Portugal+	10,374,822
Hungary+	9,849,000
Sweden+	9,747,355
Austria+	8,584, 926
Bulgaria+	7,202,198
Denmark+	5,659,715
Finland+	5,471, 753
Slovakia+	5,421,349

Ireland+	4,625,885
Croatia+	4,225, 316
Slovenia+	2,062,874
Latvia+	1,986,096
Estonia+	1,313,271
Cyprus+	847,008
Luxembourg+	562,958
Malta+	429, 344
Total:	**508,191,116**

From the above a curious anomaly emerges; Romania, for example, has 1,309 members working within the Brussels arena, while Britain has 1,187. Romania has a population of almost 20 million. Britain's population is 65 million. France's population is not much larger at 66 million, yet their representation within the EU is nearly 10% of the workforce; 3,233 officials, representatives and staff, nearly three times larger.

Britain is not a member of the 'euro club' and we still have our own currency. But this fact should mean *we* need better representation, while France, with Brussels on the doorstep and as a fully-fledged euro currency user, should need *less*.

Or doesn't it work like that?

WHAT IS THE BEST PLAN FOR BRITAIN?

It's is clear from any perspective that The EU is a vast, byzantine organisation of such complexity and cost that it cannot be considered as a viable economic, social or political entity.

Its brief history demonstrates that it cannot control its own budget (for many years no respected accounting professional would even endorse the yearly figures). Politically it has been a disaster – the problem of Greece remains unresolved, except that the Greek population has to live with consequences of an ill-advised bid for membership. They would have been better off alone.

This may be true for other nations, as well. No structure was put in place to deal with defaults or currency fluctuations impacting on nations with GDP far below that of lead nation, Germany. Feeble administration and lack of planning failed to establish external borders while encouraging the Shengen agreement on open borders internally; grand gestures with little substance and disastrous consequences.

Britain's 'special case' is an oddball from the EU perspective. Their instinct is to control, especially to control Britain's laissez faire economic philosophy, one that works. The EU is keen to hamper Britain's place as a leader in financial markets, hi-tech and medical pioneering. Instinctively, France and Germany see Britain's global reach as a threat; they will (and do) use EU legislation to diminish our influence.

Britain is a magnet for immigration. The back-door entry via further 'open-border' or 'shared-responsibility' pressure is another device to neutralise Britain's economy and influence. In a small island – half the size of France but with a comparable population – further immigration of poorly skilled workers will place a huge burden on already stretched financial resources. The attraction for all is that, in the UK, anyone can 'learn English'. This is the great cultural prize that many see as the passport to a job anywhere in the world. The UK is a 'special case' which Europe fails to recognise. From inside the EU, (this information based on 30 years' observing and monitoring) everything points to an unavoidable conclusion:

1) The EU is a huge, unwieldy institution. It is poorly governed and too large to be 'fit for purpose'. Though theoretically, 'democratic', in reality, central governance is remote and inflexible to representation.
2) Internal exchange of information is not a 'two-way street'; EU citizens are bludgeoned by authoritarian dictate, but there's no 'return channel' for either groups or individuals to express their view.
3) To 'work for the EU' is common European ambition; that way you have a secure job for life, expenses for travel and accommodation. It's practically impossible to sack anyone who works for the EU and incompetence and poor results are overlooked or 'lost to view'. 'Citizens pick up the tab'. The 'tab' is escalating.
4) While this system works for the core members, it is costly, inefficient and murderously slow; tabled legislation can take years to put into effect, by which time everything has changed and the rulings already obsolete. Nevertheless,

legislation goes ahead because of the unwritten law: the EU cannot be wrong, cannot fail.

5) As in agriculture, fishing, worker's rights, consumer rights or any other field of endeavour, the procedure of the EU is so leaden that any legislation is almost guaranteed to be redundant within the time-scale taken for implementation.

6) And does the UK really want to stay in a 'club' and await the next 'intake' (listed above) when these will place even greater burdens financially and impose further restrictions and delays on effective legislation?

7) The EU is flying in the face of modern methodology in business and government; smaller, leaner, more professional groupings are becoming the norm. They are less of a burden for their populations, better for civil action, destined to distribute better the rewards for co-operative effort.

8) Already the EU is a dinosaur – growing bigger and heavier by the year, unfit to encourage the potential of member nations. Instead it is a politically and economically flawed group, none with the confidence to stand alone and hiding up each other's failures.

9) The EU will do everything in its power to make sure legislation impacts the UK disproportionately. The UK is seen as a serious competitor in world markets and for global influence. What better way to 'neutralise' Britain, but to make sure its wings are clipped. Among the few, the UK dutifully 'plays by the rules'.

10) We don't need the EU. We have the business brains and the skills to stand on our own; the very thing that irks the EU.

YOUR VOTING CHOICES....

The people of Great Britain and the United Kingdom now – at last – have the chance to decide the future direction for their country. Continuing membership means that chance will be lost forever.

...THIS MAY BE YOUR VERY LAST CHANCE

The EU may fail. If not, it will have to grow ever-larger and become more unwieldy. It will not become fairer, more democratic, more efficient, more 'user friendly'; rather the reverse.

Voting to remain:

Increasing size as further nations join will mean more costs, more migration within the EU. Britain's status as a member Nation but 'opting out' will be increasingly challenged. Prosperity for UK will diminish, not increase. EU Legislation is intended to diminish Britain's status

Many commercial groups and business have only their profit margins and yields to consider: There is no advantage for their customers – benefits are to be had in internal accounting and access to markets. Many companies would welcome a single currency because accounting becomes more 'cost effective'.

Many cite travel as an advantage if the Euro became Britain's currency. In fact, put a UK bank card in a cash Machine anywhere in the EU, and Euros are dispensed. You can use a bank card from UK wherever you go; hotels, filling stations, shops, restaurants. Any experienced traveller knows this.

Voting for freedom from EU bureaucracy.

The EU costs a huge amount every year. We'll save billions every year, money well spent on hospitals, infrastructure and schools.

Businesses will welcome the option to be in Europe but not part of the draconian E.U legal system, with ineffective and complex legislation. The UK is right on the doorstep but open to business for the US and the rest of the world as well as Europe. Many companies will find Britain as the ideal place to be.

British identity will be protected: our customs, language, currency, law as well as our sovereignty and increasingly rare identity as a historic nation.

Nations worldwide respect and admire Britain as a Democracy, a nation to be emulated. They come to learn, they come as tourists, they come as workers and as traders, as businesses and scholars. We must preserve our unique position in the world.

*"Like a failing supermarket,
the EU has had its day.
The bills and the queues
get longer and longer.
Meanwhile, the town dies."*

BEYOND PRICE

Unique Britain – Let's Keep It That Way.

30 Years of Monitoring Britain's EU Membership

Editions Villecroze, 83690, Var, Cote d'Azure, France.